Why do some kids have freckles?

Disney BOOKS BY MAIL

DK Direct Limited
Managing Art Editor Eljay Crompton
Senior Editor Rosemary McCormick
Writer Alexandra Parsons
Illustrators The Alvin White Studios and Richard Manning
Designers Amanda Barlow, Veneta Bullen, Richard Clemson,
Sarah Goodwin, Diane Klein, Sonia Whillock

Contents

How many bones do we have?

It depends how old you are! A baby has 300 bones, but by the time a baby grows up the number has gone down to 206. This is not because bones get lost along the way, but because many tiny bones join together as we grow.

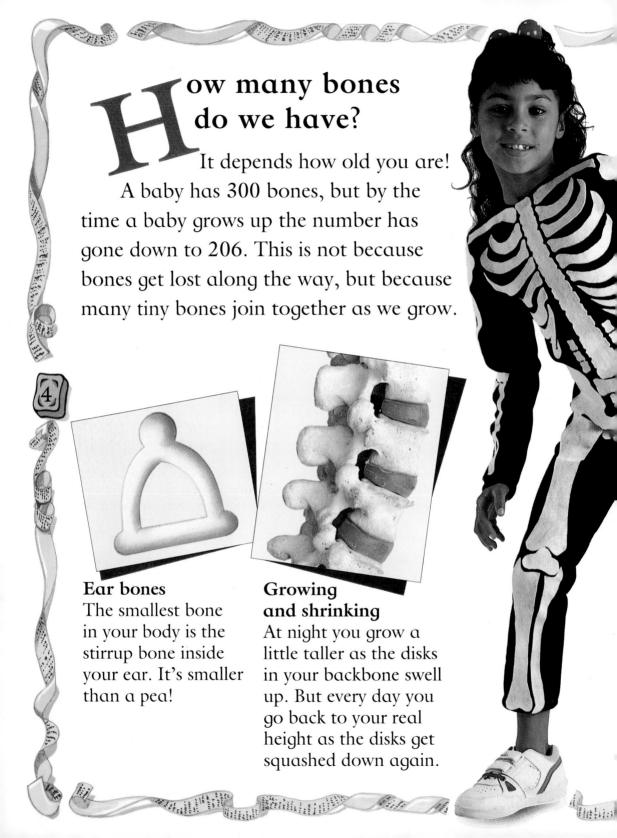

Ear bones
The smallest bone in your body is the stirrup bone inside your ear. It's smaller than a pea!

Growing and shrinking
At night you grow a little taller as the disks in your backbone swell up. But every day you go back to your real height as the disks get squashed down again.

A skeleton joke
Why couldn't Freddy the skeleton go to the store?
Because he had no body to go with him!

5

Bony facts

☞ The thigh bone, or femur, is the longest and strongest bone in your body.

☞ Bones aren't solid. They have a spongy inside so they are strong but not too heavy.

☞ A piece of bone no bigger than your thumb could support a small truck.

Why do we get two sets of teeth?

You have one set of baby teeth for a baby-size mouth. Then when you're five or six years old, your mouth has grown so much, it needs a bigger set of teeth. So your baby teeth start to fall out to make room for your new teeth, called adult teeth.

No gaps!
Humans get only two sets, but a lot of animals get as many sets of teeth as they need. If a shark loses a tooth – no problem – it just grows another one!

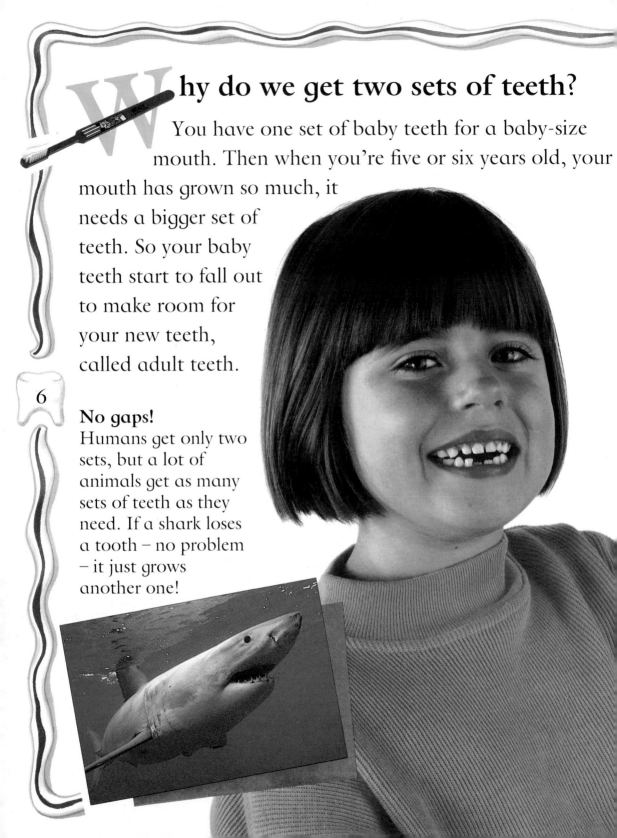

Toothy tales

👉 To "have a sweet tooth" means you love to eat sweet things like cake and candy.

👉 We have flat teeth at the back of our mouth for grinding food, called molars. We have sharp teeth at the front for cutting, called incisors.

👉 When they are in their twenties, most grown-ups get four more back teeth, called wisdom teeth.

Why do we yawn when we are tired?

Because our bodies need more oxygen. If you're feeling sleepy, or you've been sitting still for a long time, your brain will tell your body to yawn so that you gulp in a big mouthful of fresh air filled with oxygen.

Aaaaaaaah! Cats, even big ones, yawn and stretch a lot because they spend so much time curled up snoozing.

Copycat

Yawning can be catching, but nobody quite knows why. If you see someone else yawning, doesn't it make you want to yawn, too?

Airy facts

☞ A 15-year-old girl once yawned for five weeks without stopping.

☞ When you're asleep, you take about one breath every three or four seconds.

☞ During a race, you would need 15 times as much oxygen as you do when you're resting.

Why do some kids have freckles?

Probably because their mother or father had freckles, too. Freckles are little brown spots that people with pale skin and red hair often have. Hair and skin color are passed down through genes from parents to their children.

To Junior
love Mom
and Dad
X X

TO JUNIOR,
SUMMER CAMP,
LAKESIDE!

The gene that makes you short is stronger than the gene that makes you tall.

The genes for curly hair and brown eyes are stronger than the genes for straight hair and blue eyes.

MOM

DAD

Whose genes are those?

Genes (not jeans) are little messages tucked away inside our bodies that make us grow up to look, and act, the way we do. We get genes from our parents, and some genes are stronger than others.

What happens to the food we eat?

Once you've chewed it and swallowed it, food travels down into your stomach. From there it goes on a long journey through your intestines. During this journey, food is changed from solid to mush, and all the things that are good for you are soaked into the body to give it energy.

Down the hatch!

The balloons in this picture show where your food goes after you've swallowed it. Food can take up to two days to travel through your body.

Eat up!

The average person will munch his or her way through 50 tons of food in a lifetime. That's the same weight as three elephants – yikes!

Food facts

☞ The liver is one of the organs that soaks in the nutrients from the food you eat. It stores vitamins and other good things until they're needed.

☞ A sip of milk will take around six seconds to reach your tummy.

Why do we shiver when it's cold?

To warm ourselves up! If you get very cold, the temperature of your body will drop. Then your brain knows you're cold, so it sends messages to your nerves, telling them to twitch your muscles to get them moving to warm you up a little.

Airy fur
The arctic fox keeps warm because its fur stands on end, trapping a layer of warm air next to its skin.

Keeping warm
Eskimos know a thing or two about trapping warm air inside their clothes. They put on several thin layers of clothes first, and then they wear furry clothes on top with the fur side facing inside.

Shivery facts

Did you know that we lose most of our body heat through our head? So, when it's cold outside, remember to put a woolly hat on.

Fingers, toes, and lips have many nerve endings and are some of the most sensitive parts of our body. That's why they go numb when it's cold.

15

What happens when we breathe?

Air fills our lungs, and tiny blood vessels in our lungs take in a gas from the air called oxygen. Our blood carries oxygen around to every part of our body. Our body needs oxygen to keep it going.

Spongy lungs
Our lungs are a spongy mixture of tubes, bubbles, and blood vessels. They get bigger when we breathe in and smaller when we breathe out.

IN

OUT

Puff, puff!
When you exercise, your body needs more oxygen. The harder you exercise, the faster your breathing gets.

Gasp, gasp!
The higher up you go toward the sky, the less oxygen there is in the air. That's why on mountain tops people get breathless and have to breathe more deeply.

17

Breathtaking facts

☞ The air we breathe out has less oxygen in it than the air we breathe in. That's because our body has used most of it up.

☞ The human body can stay alive three weeks without food but only a few minutes without oxygen.

Why do some people have gray hair?

Hair contains color cells, that's why people have different color hair like red, brown, black, and blond. As you grow older, the color in the color cells gets weaker. When there is very little color left, hair looks gray and when all the color has gone, it looks white.

Hair-raising
Your hair has no feeling and it keeps on growing even if you dye it, frizz it, or curl it!

Hair ha ha!
What did one ear say to the other ear?
Between us we need a haircut.

Curly locks

It's those genes again! If your mom or dad have curly hair, then you'll probably have curls, too.

19

Hairy facts

☞ We lose and replace 100 hairs every day.

☞ Your hair grows faster in the morning than at night.

☞ You have about 100,000 hairs on your head.

What happens when we dream?

Dreams are the brain's way of sorting out any new things we've learned, or any experiences we've had during the day. If you are feeling sad, or if you are looking forward to something, it will often appear in your dreams.

Dream Time

Dreams last about half an hour. You'll have about four dreams a night, but you probably won't remember them.

Do animals dream?

Yes. You can tell when animals dream because you can see their eyelids fluttering as the eyeballs underneath move very quickly. Cats spend more time dreaming about chasing mice than actually chasing them!

Dreamy facts

You will spend about one-third of your life asleep. Imagine how many dreams you'll have!

Scientists think that babies dream when they're still inside their mothers.

A man from Chicago had the longest dream ever recorded in a laboratory. His dream lasted more than two hours.

What does blood do?

Blood is the body's transportation system. It keeps the body supplied with everything it needs and takes away anything it doesn't. It picks up oxygen from the lungs, and energy-giving food from the stomach. In fact, it visits every part of the body except our hair and nails.

Listen to that beat!

Blood is kept moving around the body by the heart, which is like a pump. You can hear your heart beat as it pumps your blood.

What happens when we blush?

When we feel embarrassed, our brain sends signals to the nerves in our face. The nerves tell the blood vessels in our cheeks to get bigger, and we end up with a bright red face!

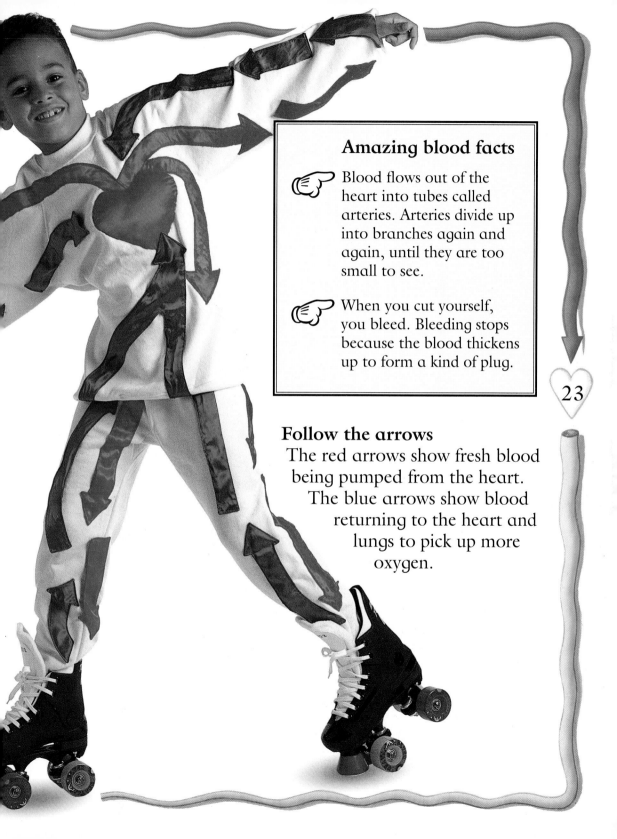

Amazing blood facts

☞ Blood flows out of the heart into tubes called arteries. Arteries divide up into branches again and again, until they are too small to see.

☞ When you cut yourself, you bleed. Bleeding stops because the blood thickens up to form a kind of plug.

23

Follow the arrows

The red arrows show fresh blood being pumped from the heart. The blue arrows show blood returning to the heart and lungs to pick up more oxygen.

How do we catch a cold?

We don't catch colds, they catch us! There are over 100 different little cold viruses zipping around looking for a new nose to settle in.

Cold busters
A cold is a fight between your body and one of those viruses. A healthy diet helps you to win that fight, so eat your fruit and vegetables!

Hold on to your hat!
The breeze from a sneeze can reach 60 m.p.h. That's faster than most speed limits on the highway.

A sick joke
Patient: "Doctor, doctor, I keep thinking I'm invisible!"
Doctor: "Who said that?"

24

Cold facts

☞ Hundreds of years ago, in Europe, people believed that when their nose was running it meant their brain was leaking!

☞ We get a lot of colds in winter because we stay indoors more with other people. Then we catch viruses from each other.

Why do we have skin?

To keep our insides in and germs and dirt out. Skin also stops us from drying out. There is a lot of water in the human body, and if we had no skin we'd dry up like prunes.

Close your eyes!

Your skin is where your sense of touch is. It is full of nerve endings that send messages back to your brain. Even with your eyes closed, you can still tell what you're touching. Try it using a sponge, a stone, and a piece of ice.

26

Soaps up!

Mom is right when she says it's important to keep clean. We need to wash away dirt and to get rid of dead skin cells that hang around on the surface of our skin. If we didn't, we would look and smell yucky!

Skinny facts

☞ You get a whole new skin every 50 days.

☞ Your skin weighs twice as much as your brain.

☞ Skin also helps to keep your body at the right temperature.

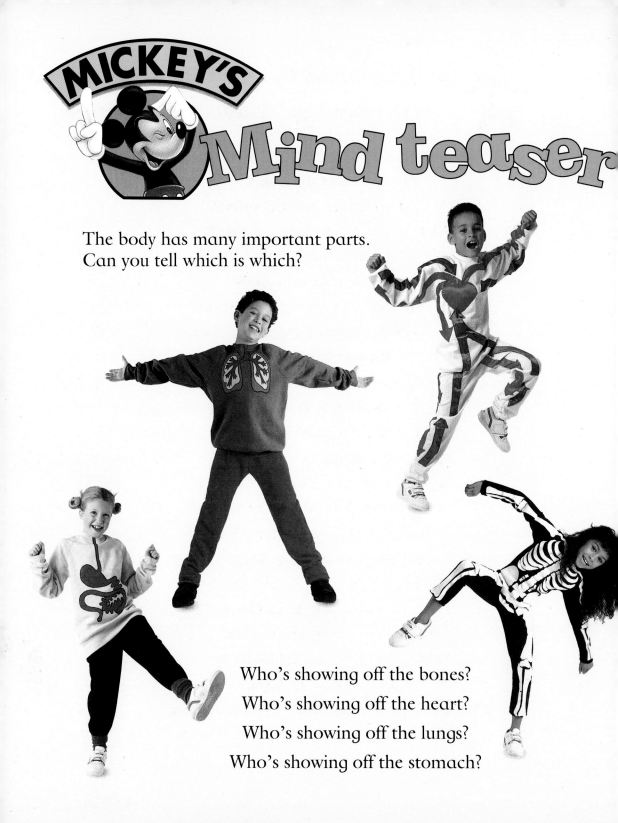

MICKEY'S Mind teaser

The body has many important parts.
Can you tell which is which?

Who's showing off the bones?
Who's showing off the heart?
Who's showing off the lungs?
Who's showing off the stomach?